"The Story Behind the Words: My Journey"
Volume I & Volume II

By

J. Patrick, Esq.

**Edited and Illustrated by
Delma "Pebbles" Hogan**

Table of Contents

Legal Notes	IV
Disclaimer	V
About The Author	VI
Prologue	IX
Mother Root	XII
My Queen	XVII
Why?	XXII
Dreamer	XXVI
Penthouse 62	XXIX
The People's Cry	XXXV
Salute	XXXVIII
Time	XLI
Poetry	XLV
Can I Have an Audience?	XLVIII
Love Should Be Easy	LI
Cupid	LX
People in Love	LXV
Love Doesn't Follow Any Rules	LXVIII
What Is Trust?	LXXVI

I Believe	LXXVIII
Every Family Has a Little Jerry Springer	LXXXIV
J. Patrick's Positive Change Advice	LXXXVIII
Nutrition and Fitness	XCIII
More Advice from J. Patrick, Esq.	XCVIII
The Truth	CII
Enlighten Me Not	CVII
I Believe in You	CXVI
I Win	CXIX
Walking and Content	CXXII
Saturday's Child	CXXIV
Twenty-five Years and Still Crying	CXXVI
Home, Sweet Home!	CXXVIII
My Famous Quotes	CXXXII
Readers' Quotes	CXL

Legal Notes

Copyright © 2015

All rights reserved. No part of this book may be reproduced, stored in a retrieval system, or transmitted in any form or by any means, electronic, mechanical, photocopying, recording, scanning, or otherwise, without the prior written permission of the publisher.

Disclaimer

All the material contained in this book is provided for educational and informational purposes only. No responsibility can be taken for any results or outcomes resulting from the use of this material.

While every attempt has been made to provide information that is both accurate and effective, the author does not assume any responsibility for the accuracy or use/misuse of this information.

About The Author

J. Patrick, Esquire began writing at an early age. He traveled extensively as a child into adulthood, which in no doubt, contributed to his diverse and broad outlook on life. His style of writing is as unique and exceptional as he.

Mr. Patrick has the natural gift to conceptualize an idea and bring it to fruition. His consulting prowess is second to none. One of his passions is to assist others by helping them advance to the next level. He would rather teach an individual how to fish, rather than give him a fish. If the proper tools and guidance are supplied; then, one can succeed in life. This principle is foundational and necessary for success; and, he stands by it.

Sharing his heart through words on paper comes naturally to him. But, he will be the first to tell you there is someone else behind the passages that unfold from his thoughts. He takes no glory from Him.

J. Patrick's signature line says it all:

"I am not the author, just the vessel."

About the Illustrator

Delma "Pebbles" Hogan is a Graphic Designer from Fort Pierce, Florida. In 2014, after over twenty years in the Accounting/Payroll fields, she decided to go full time as an entrepreneur. She is thankful for the gifts that God has blessed her with; and, she uses all of them to bring her clients' dreams to life.

Prologue

My friend, may I call you my friend? I might get off of the subject a little and ramble. This is what happens when you're trying to figure things out (me and my mental breakdown).

Have you ever asked yourself, "What is my purpose? How did I get myself in this position (the rat race)?"

Do you like who you are?

"I thought so!

We have become creatures of habit. What happened to laughter? When did everything get so serious? We've defined ourselves by status, or by what we do or do not have. I have learned that you can have everything and still be unhappy. If something can be taken from you, then it's not yours.

Be brutally honest. Are you happy? Another question, Why not?

I ask a lot of questions.

You're not obligated to read this book. The reason for which I wrote the book is simple. I am trying to understand myself. If you have a problem with that, then put the book down.

I notice you're still reading. Let's address some simple issues we have inside. We are a society of unhappy, discontented people. We are an entitlement generation.

Another question, can you love someone and not like their character?

If you let bad decisions cultivate your future, then you will never be happy.

Let's make a list together.

Mother Root

Chapter 1

This chapter is dedicated to my mother, Yvonne Joy Phillips.

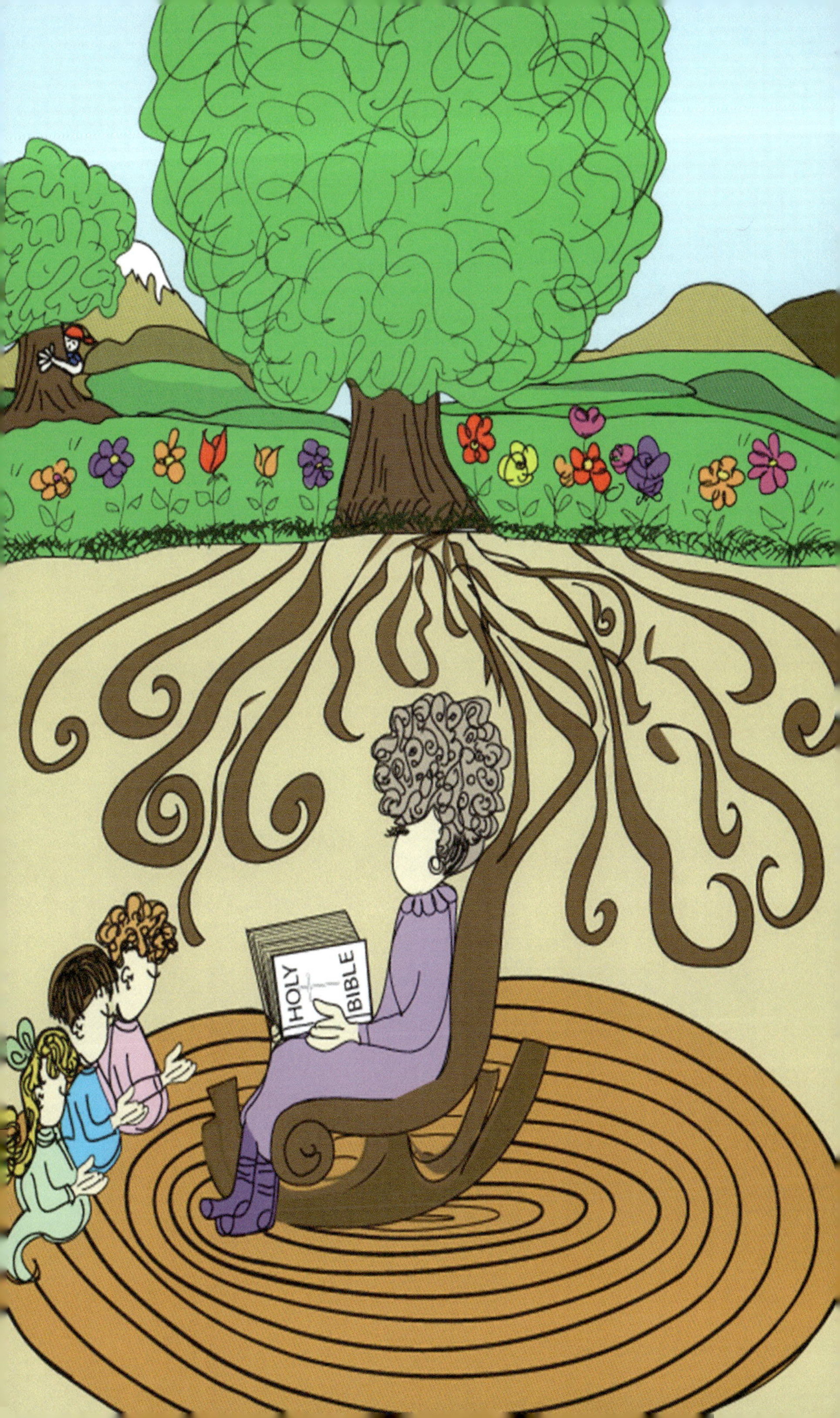
HOLY
BIBLE

Mother Root

"Mother Root" is not that easy to talk about. This was a very emotional situation for my mom. You are talking to a mama's boy. Back in the day, I was a real mama's boy!

It was a Saturday morning around 10:14 A.M., maybe 10: 20 A.M., somewhere around that; after the gym, where I was getting my sexy on, I went to see her. She was a little under the weather because a family member had said something about her that got her very upset. This person said, "She brought us to this country and she thinks we owe her for life! Who does she think she is?" Wow, that was a low blow to my mom's ego. I watched her sacrifice blood, sweat, and tears for her family. A lot of them never even said thank you. This hurt her deeply since everything she did was out of love; and, all she got back was animosity. Wow!!! That's family for you!

Mom, I love you, anyway.

I see you're planting.
Look how strong your people have grown.
As I sit here wondering, "Why they hold the rain and block the sun?"
Don't they understand your roots are very strong?
The rich soil and water runs very deep.
How can you work around the clock in a dusty, parched land and still have gentle hands?
Never fear the wind even when it blows so hard.
O, Mother Root, look how your seeds are so strong; when weeds run wild and die so young.

A fruitless plant with no nourishment;
all they have in mind is self-fulfillment and destruction.
O, Mother Root, look how your seeds are so strong;
this is the opportunity to tell your story;
how you sacrifice and cultivate with the direction of your mighty hand.
The greatest healer I ever met; my mother, my sister, my history.
Like the red peeling bark of the Gumbo Limbo tree lifeline to feed the world with wisdom, direction and with a little simple history.
Bone of my bones, eye of my eyes, smile of my smiles;
That's the only thing she says to me.
She did it all for her family!

My Queen

Chapter 2

XVIII

My Queen

This might make some people upset. I was making fun of women; how they believe everything they say is right. Even though most times they are; but, can we move on? You know what, "No comment!"

My queen, yes, you are so right.

Ladies are first.

If you say jump,

I must reply, "How high?"

When will I learn

that you are so right.

Today is a new day, women's rights.

You don't need a man.

You have a job, money,

a house; and, you're very educated.

Batteries are cheap these days.

They come in all different shapes and sizes.

Today is a new day; women's rights.

All you need is

Ben and Franklin; and, with your brother's tamer in hand,

also called Smith & Wesson.

All the men in your life

ain't right;

Except Tyrone with his flamboyance and

his peculiar modern family life.

My queen, you're so right.

Why are we having this conversation?

xx

Because, you're so right?

Oh, just for peace of mind.

Today is a new day, women's rights.

She said that I am full of it.

Give me five minutes or two.

As I walk away, wow, she is right,

as I completed number two.

Why?

Chapter 3

WHY?

The ability to understand and share the feelings of another; empathy.

If I paint a picture for you; you will still not be able to understand me. If you walk in my shoes; you still will not be able to carry my burden. Your perception will always be different. You cannot have the same experience that I have.

Water is water. Fire is fire.

Everything must be logical for me; but, I am emotional. Everything must be emotional for you; but, you are logical.

It's still not the same.

Destiny Road

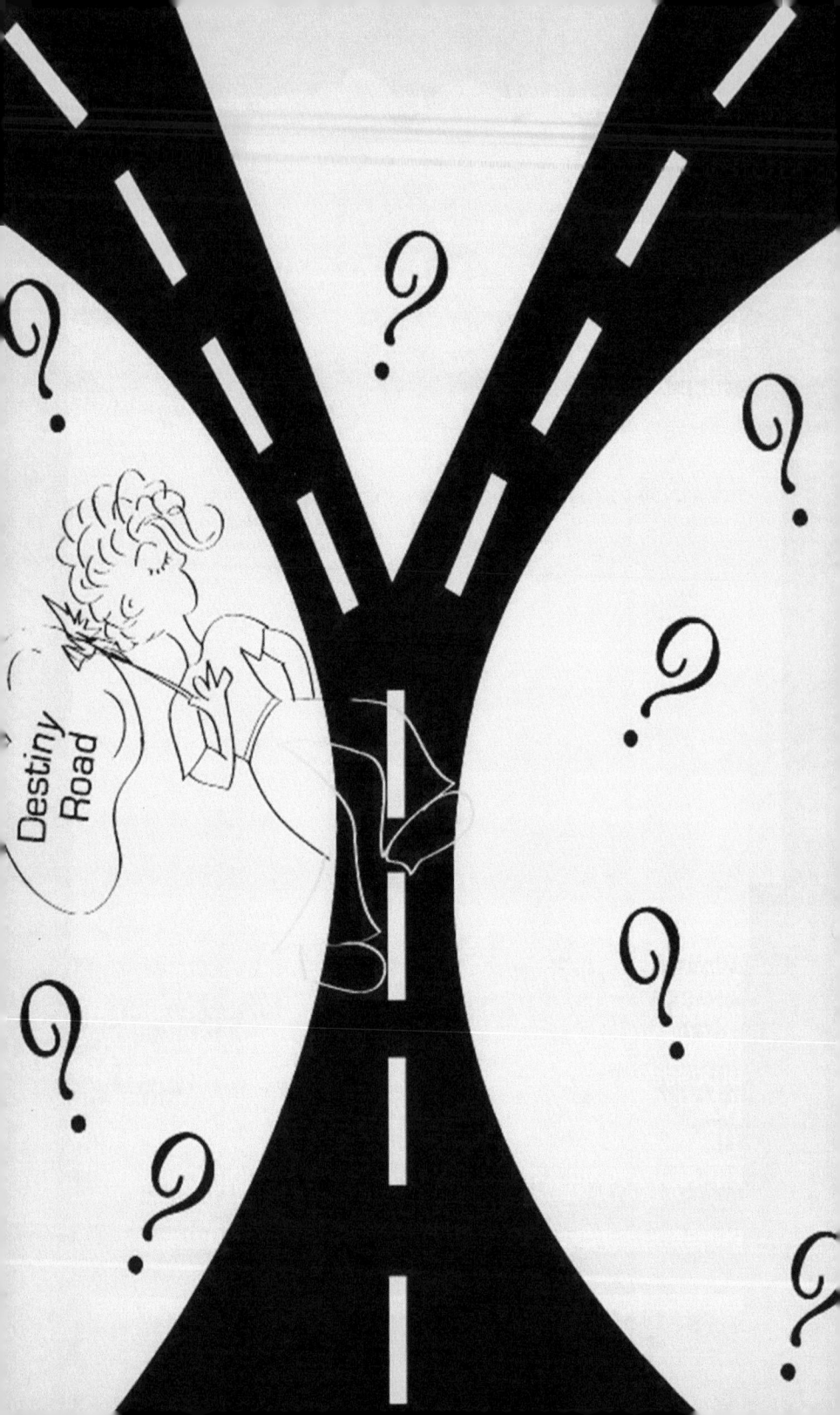

Why would the fish tell the eagle how to fly, when they've never felt the wind so high?

Why would the eagle tell the fish how to swim, when they've never swam so deep?

Why would the rain tell the sun where to shine, when it's so perfectly in line with the earth?

Why would the sun tell the rain where to fall, when it's so perfectly in line with the lake?

How can you tell me who to be when divinity was told to me?

Now, can you drop that stone?

Dreamer

Chapter 4

Dreamer

If you look at my past business venture, it was horrible. Not having the right tools or the understanding of S.M.A.R.T. goals[1], I was a joker trying to conquer the world with jesters on my team.

I've learned so much over the years that the classroom was not able to teach me. I've learned what not to do. I have a PhD in failure. Thank you, life. Now, I am strong; so, I give advice to someone else. I am king of all kings; they will prosper from my loss.

Dreamers are made with thoughts of strong passion with no action.

Winners are made with a keen sense of adjustment to losing.

Successes are made with more preparation than opportunity with thoughts of, yes, I can.

Forwardness is made with one footstep in front of the other with all the right tools.

Whatever you think of yourself, you're absolutely right!

"Today is a new day"

Penthouse 62
"The Last Song"

Chapter 5

Penthouse 62
"The Last Song"

One of my favorite pastimes is watching the History channel. A documentary about Bob Marley, aka Nesta, peeked my interest. When Nesta came on the scene, he was a "powerhouse" who was able to move mountains with a song. His songs were about the emancipation of your mind, liberation and freedom. "I Shot the Sheriff"[2] (but I didn't shoot no deputy) is one of my favorite songs of all time.

Have you ever asked yourself, "Who shot the deputy? And, why? (Research time) I was really impressed; a man with a mic, a vision and a guitar weighing less than 145 pounds dripping wet, being hated by men with influence and money. Why, you ask? Well, it was

xxx

simple. Nesta was able to control the masses with his songs. He made people question who they were.

The best way to change a man is to change his thought processes. Gandhi said it the best, watch "...your thoughts..."[3] (Another homework assignment.) We had another rising prince, Garnett Silk; but, also short lived when he met his demise in a fire trying to save a family member. (No comment.)

Nesta was diagnosed with cancer after seeking medical attention from a football (soccer) injury. He went to Germany for treatment to no avail. On his return to the states, he checked into Cedars Hospital in Miami[4] and was assigned, Penthouse 62. In Penthouse 62, I wonder what his last thoughts, his last song was. I visualize it as the Last Supper, his closest friends and family at his bedside all passing a "big head spliff". When a man can accept his transition with death, death has no power.

To my brother Bob Marley, since you can't sing your last tune, I will sing it for you.

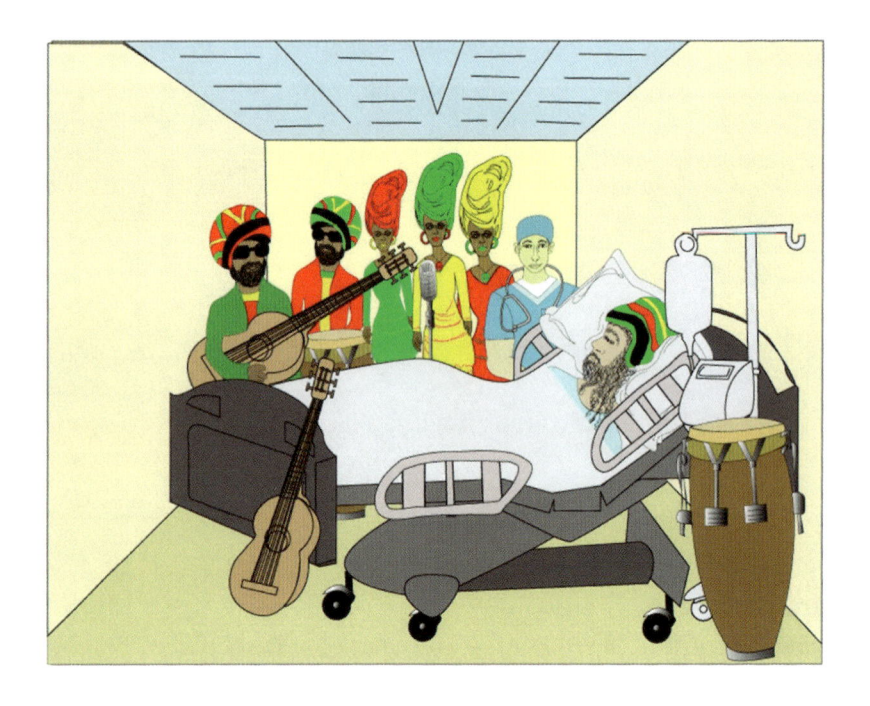

I just had a revelation, where life is the professor

and I'm one of his pupils.

As studious as I am,

I notice I am not able to believe in everything that I've seen.

I notice I am not able to believe in everything that I've heard.

So, in death I will learn the Almighty truth.

Whenever the grim reaper plays my song, it will be my final tune.

My time in this form will be over.

I will be ready with my Father in mind.

The truth will reveal itself to me;

That is Jah's truth and His understanding.

I will understand the wickedness of the world

if I believe in my Father's teachings.

My brother I must forgive;

So, that I might have a place beside Him with no regret.

Jah, knows!

This is the last tune, Almighty Jah.

I was born in a lawless land where people walk with a Bible in their hand, and, not in their heart.

Almighty Jah!

The People's Cry

Chapter 6

The People's Cry

Dear Privileged,

I have just lost, the best part of me, in a single moment. When words are not able to explain my loss, I will explain it to you.

It's like counting every drop in the ocean, and then it rains.

It's like picking up every grain of sand in the desert, and then the wind blows.

Then, you will understand my pain.

Don't put salt into our open wound, so that you can distance yourself from your involvement. I am in agreement, that things happen; but, I have just lost the best part of me, in a single moment.

    P.S.   R.I.P. MY FALLEN BROTHER AND SISTER "BlackLivesMatter"[5]

Salute

Chapter 7

This chapter is dedicated to my friend, David Merritt.

Salute

Stand up, my soldiers.

Will you stand up my soldiers?

In our presence, we have a fallen soldier.

In the morning, the rain will come to wash away our tears.

In the morning, the rain will come to wash away our fears.

Fallen soldier, it was your time.

In the afterlife, we will meet again, fallen soldier.

Until that time comes, we stand.

Fallen soldier, we release you from your duty into the Lord's hand.

Remaining soldiers, salute our fallen brother.

Remaining soldiers, salute.

XL

Time

Chapter 8

Time

There are 3,600 seconds in an hour. I work night shift; worst thing I ever did. My mother lives 2 miles away; didn't visit her for one year. Happy medium is an art form with you, time. Juggling family and work in my world; I am not one with that privilege.

If you have a lot time on your hands, then that's a red flag that you're broke. Work hard and you're broke with things. Having your relationship take a back burner so you can prosper; and, lose everything (family) for the American dream. You're broke.

There is always tomorrow for love. Now, you're stupid, broke and have child support. Only one thing good came out of it; you became a poet.

There is time we shall share.

There is time my schedule will not allow me to be there.

Even though I shall wish,

I hope you will be happy with a gentle kiss.

Precious time has passed;

I hope our love and friendship will last.

If you know the part to play, you'll learn

so much in just one short day.

Poetry

Chapter 9

XLVI

Poetry

When we talk about poetry, it's not that complicated. It makes you cry. It makes you happy. It brings emotion out of you that you don't realize you have. It makes you wonder and question who you are. It has the ability to transform you into a tree. It makes you beautiful. Everything is beautiful in poetry. It doesn't matter how much it makes you cry. You can write about the wind and actually feel the wind on your face...that's poetry.

Can I Have an Audience?

Chapter 10

XLVIII

Can I Have an Audience?

Can I have an audience, my love?

With sweet thoughts and endless precious words,

this day came with one thing in mind.

It was the beginning of a new day

when the wind blew and whispered the

sound of a mockingbird in the spring;

The rainbow followed the rain;

and, the stars followed the sunset.

I searched for you.

Yes, I did;

until I found you with this endless smile and a glow of

relief.

One thing I do know, I found you. It was a glorious day.

That day,

Praise the Lord, He favored me unconditionally. In His

name, all things are possible.

I love you.

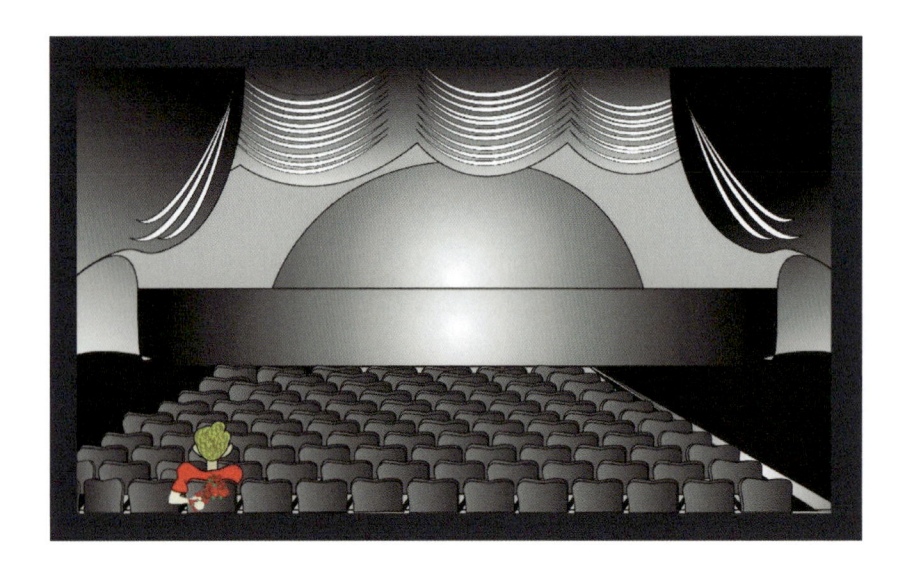

L

Love Should Be Easy

Chapter 11

Love Should Be Easy

I was going to let this one slip by without a commentary; but, Pebbles, my illustrator, wanted me to narrate this one. So, I asked myself, "How can you hate someone and love them at the same time. Living in South Florida, I witness rainy days with blue skies; the sun out shining, hot.

My story is nothing new under the sun. Now I am singing, "*It's a Thin Line Between Love and Hate.*"[6] Are you hungry?

I had some bad relationships; some directly and

indirectly my fault. Being young and restless made me about that life. I made a lot of bad decisions. I learned that you shouldn't eat ice with a toothache. And, that it's okay to be a young fool; but, not an old one.

It was not always that way. I wanted it all. I gave it all. As years went by, my bad habits became my norm. Karma came with a big bag to cash my check. Be happy I don't speak French!

I realized I was in love. I would rather accept death over a broken heart. I cried inside with no tears, not understanding why. You would have thought I was a lottery winner the way I checked my phone.

I was in the clouds counting sheep; trying to sleep. I

see why alcohol and depression went together, hand in hand; if you call Seagram's alcohol. I am not big on drinking. Today was a new day.

I became my worst enemy. I was slowly killing myself with my thoughts. *"It's a Thin Line Between Love and Hate."*[6] I knew better; yet, I was still hopeless. What did I do wrong? How can I fix it? O, my God, this! O, my God, that!

It was the first time I hated everyone around me; especially, the man in the mirror.

Wow, another seven years of bad luck!
This particular night, I had a lot on my mind. How do I find closure? So, I had the bright idea of driving to the beach. (Key West) What was I thinking (about three hours later)? Driving all this way in the dark trying to

catch the sunrise. (I have this special thing for sunrises and sunsets.) I wonder how that's going to play out someday. Will the sunrise catch me?

It is so beautiful on this long 7-mile bridge. When you are by yourself, you think a lot about everything...the madness. I read somewhere that Virgos think a lot. I'm a real Virgo...an alpha male. With my mindset and built up emotions, I have the capability to do many bad things. What makes it worse is knowing the right people who think the same way. (I'm a wolf.) You let your emotions build up; now, you're a time-bomb ticking. Fortunately, that was another whole life; and, I'm pleased that I chose not to take the way of self-destruction. God is my witness. My friend, never become an irrational and dangerous person. This is how you end up on *I.D.* (The Investigation Discovery TV Show). I'm happy that I decided to tread a different path.

At the lowest point of my life, I'm in the Keys. The Keys have changed a lot. I barely recognized it. I wonder what Ernest Hemingway would say if he could see it now. Rest in Peace; I'll be your eyes. It has lost its serenity; but, the beach is still beautiful. The birds are still happy; that's a plus. The wind is still gentle and the salt air cleans out your sinuses. I've got to fix that one day. Water does something to one's true nature. I understand why people love it so.

I have a precious gift for the ocean. Most people would look at the face value of it; but, not the sentimental destruction. I had to detach myself from it and all the demons that came with it. There is no one to blame, but myself. Most people would think I am insane; but, I am not most people. When you become your worst enemy, then you will understand. I took my ex-girlfriend's engagement ring; I took a deep breath; and 1, 2, 3…there it goes…blip, like a fish. Wow! It was easier than I thought. You think I would be upset; but, I wasn't. Now, I have to work extra shifts to put the money back into my 401K, $ 4,500 to be exact, plus what I added to it. It was a costly lesson. I'm a guy; we are stupid.

Driving home was easy. It was like the calm before the storm. I didn't understand; but, who am I to question it? No one even realized that I went out town, except my smart phone. As I drove into my driveway, it responded to me, "You're home." Big brother is watching us. This is crazy.

If the sun gets too hot, it will burn out and turn cold. That is the law of physics. My pain was so deep until it turned into laughter… ha, ha, ha. My friend will you laugh with me?

Love should be easy;

All I see is the pain.

Love should be beautiful;

All I see is the ugliness.

Love should be right;

All I can see is the wrong.

Love should be peaceful;

All I can see is the drama.

Love should be a joke;

Then, we would be able to partake in the

Laughter and dance with the jester.

Cupid

Chapter 12

CUPID

Women are conditioned to believe that men are emotionless; and, that we don't care. That is not the full story. We are driven by the power of alpha vs. alpha. We don't care what women think; even if it's in our best interest. Why should we have to learn the words, "'yes, dear', 'how high', and 'okay boss'", to be happy? We will choose the worst over quality; ruin our lives over it; and, take a life time trying to fix it.

I've encountered the sexiest chick with the worst morals in the world; and, she is bipolar happy. That's why the ones who listen to their women win. We are confused; and, we love the game. Never want to be normal. We want to be exceptional; even if it's for 15 minutes of making it rain. (Did you pay my rent?) And, the funniest thing, envy the 9 to 5 guys with the family morals.

If you are a person who cares about what people think, then you will never be happy in the matrix of life.

We don't believe in love? That's so far from the truth. The greatest gift is true love. But, we let ego, television, and books tell us what's beautiful. What happened to beauty being in the eye of the beholder?

It's a catch 22; we have to lose everything to address our shortcomings. ("My Life of Job")

Cupid, "Where is my arrow?"

In the heart of another.

"Where is my sunshine?"

In the warmth of another.

"Where is my joy?"

In the laughter of another.

"Where is my love?"

In the hand of another.

How is this possible when

I have been waiting for so long?"

Cupid! "Can you find my arrow

With its target in line with

The scope of my heart?"

People in Love

Chapter 13

People in Love

People in love don't talk too loudly to each other.

They speak softly with a whisper because they are speaking to one another's souls; placing the other person's needs over their own.

Don't get it twisted; it's complicated.

He sold his motorcycle to buy her tires.

She sold her car to buy him a motor.

They are in a worse position than before; but not necessarily.

A fool in love; how beautiful!

Baby, you're so crazy, bah bah boo; whatever that means.

Even people in love are on the wrong page.

That's so beautiful!

Love Doesn't Follow Any Rules

Chapter 14

LXVIII

Love Doesn't Follow Any Rules

Love doesn't follow any rules. *"It's a Thin Line Between Love and Hate."*[6]   Live with it.

One of the greatest love stories was William Shakespeare's, *"Romeo and Juliet"*. Their families, the Montagues and the Capulets, forbade them to be together; however, love brought them together in death. They would choose death over living without each other. So, when you look for Mr. Right or Mrs. Right, look closely, thoroughly. Are you in love with the status or are you in love with being in love? 100% of 50, plus 100% of 50 equals 100%. That is true love completed. If you are damaged, full of baggage, or have unresolved closure, then we have some work to do. But, that's okay; you're not the only one.

True love doesn't have a title. You may ask, "What is a title?" Let's just say, when that person loses it all, you lose it all. Don't get it twisted. You were in love with the situation, not that person. Most people will never understand true love because they don't know what true love is. They are more focused on the situation. (Watching too much television or fairy tales.) Your knight in shining armor will not come on a white horse. He will come with a "Hello."; or, "Are you okay?" But, unfortunately, you will have the bad boy or bad girl complex.

If I were to ask you what is true love? You would describe possessions and titles. (i.e., Oh, he wines and dines me. He has a fancy car; a good job; and good credit. Or, she has a cute shape; or, he has a power title.) Why haven't I heard anything about he takes my breath away; or, she completes me? Come on now; let's get down and dirty like *Fifty Shades of Grey*. That is not love at all.

When you start talking about beauty, bodies, or swagger; you're talking about lust, love of possessions and love of lust. Have you ever been in a relationship and not know them at all? That happens all of the time. You were focused on the situation and not the person. (Preach, pastor! Yes, we're in church today.) Dear women, why should men buy the cow when the milk is free? Dear men, with your bad behavior, you will always lose in the end. Enough will never be enough. If you love the wrong person, you'll be singing the words from the song "*When a Man Loves a Woman*", she can do no wrong. (Yes, I know. Hey, that's my version of the song.)

What is true love? Love will always be silly with plenty of laughter. The sillier the couple, the more in love they are with one another. Conversation will not be needed. They communicate in a whisper because their hearts speak to each other. On the other hand, dialogue is needed to get to that point. With true love, the other person's needs come before their needs. She will be your weakness; and, he will be your strength. When you're in love with someone, that person can do no wrong.

Why are people together? People are together for many different reasons. If you're together to paint a picture for society, you will never be complete. Be careful of what you wish for. Regret will hurt you in your ribs. Huh? Don't go crazy, it's just a metaphor. (Remember that Eve was created from Adam's rib.)

Most people put more effort into planning the wedding than they do in building the relationship. When you bring people into your relationship, it is a relationship killer. This occurs whether you speak negatively or positively about your spouse. Yes, positivity brings jealousy. Don't forget; misery loves company. Speaking to the wrong person about your relationship can infect it like a cancer. Expressing your thoughts to a stranger would be better. Keep this in mind. After you reconcile and forgive, your family and friends are still in their feelings because they haven't forgiven that person. You must go back to family and friends and let them know that you've made it right with your spouse. You have to acknowledge your part in it. One side of the story is never the truth.

Love will take on a life of its own; it doesn't follow any rules. I didn't choose love; it chose me. If love chooses you, you will discover true love. It is not based on things. If you are damaged, you won't realize it until it's too late. Work through your issues, face them head on; and, let your heart heal. Pause for a minute. If this were your last moment, who would you think of in your last breath? I hope that wasn't too cold for you. Thank you for picking the book back up. You're probably asking, "Who am I to tell you about love?" You're right. I am not a specialist; but, I've learned what not to do.

P.S.

Story by Damaged Goods

What Is Trust?

Chapter 15

What Is Trust?

Do you have some time? Go get a piece of paper. I will wait. Go, get the paper. What's taking you so long? Okay, crumple the paper in your fist. Now straighten it out. That's trust. Tell me, how hard would it be to remove the wrinkles and make the piece of paper straight again? So, if you lie to me, I have to question every truth you have ever told. That is how you explain trust.

I Believe

Chapter 16

I Believe

In midsummer of last year, I witnessed propaganda at its finest. The media used information impartially, and primarily to influence my belief (lying by omission). They made it seem like the world was coming to an end; a little white lie. Next day I woke; the sun was still shining.

I came to accept that the world is not fair. That made me part of the problem (When good men do nothing, all is lost.) using objects of intolerance to teach tolerance; and, promote social justice. My daughter had a great day in summer camp today. She likes this little boy; I'll talk to her later.

This six letter word that controls the world, "racism". From religion to perception, you'll never understand racism until you live in America; in my particular case, E Pluribus Unum (out of many, one).[7]

When you look at my family tree, just call us gumbo; from blue black to blue vein; from A to Z and still counting. I love the blackberry. They are the sweetest. We hail from all parts of the world. No one is directly from the motherland; but, the blood is strong. There's something bad we can say about everyone; I love them all anyway.

LXXX

At work, we see the strongest warrior cry like a baby from a little pain; and, a little angel whisper to her mother, "I'll be strong for you, mom", as she takes her last breath.

My relationship with God gives me strength to wake up.

I Am RACIST AGAINST RACISM.

I believe there will be a tomorrow,

Even after tomorrow.

I believe the sun will rise and

Shine on us tomorrow.

I believe there will be peace on

EARTH one day after tomorrow.

I believe that love will conquer all,

One day after tomorrow.

I believe the Almighty will come,

One day after tomorrow.

I believe we'll be brothers,

One day after tomorrow.

LXXXII

But, today we will fight

for justice and equality; or,

there will be no more tomorrow.

Working together,

for a better tomorrow.

Every Family Has a Little Jerry Springer

Chapter 17

Every Family Has a Little Jerry Springer[8]

Knock, knock. Who is there? At my window all you can hear, with a low voice,

"Bro, let me get $20 for gas." I wake up to give it to him. In my mind, I thought it would be easy to give it to him. Stupid me; when you a feed duck, the next day there are two more.

Just call me, Mr. Enabler.

We have become a society that chooses substance over quality as the norm.
Fine china is now plastic plates.

YouTube is our teacher.

Facebook is our entertainment.

The phone is our mother and father.

Technology comes with a price, and no receipt.

I was surprised to see how much

every family has a little Jerry Springer.

The pain of truth,

Just a little Jerry Springer.

The pain of family issues,

Just a little Jerry Springer.

The pain of bad behavior,

Just a little Jerry Springer.

J. Patrick's Positive Change Advice

Chapter 18

J. Patrick's Positive Change Advice

- ➢ Love yourself first.

    The best way to lose weight is to get rid of negative people around you. Give them the pink slip. You must identify the real problem, **you**!

    Get the proper rest. Go to sleep. Remove the distractions from the bedroom; all electronics, i.e. television. Turn off the computer, cell phone, tablet and iPad.

    Opt for better nutrition and exercise.

- ➢ Communicate.

    Communication is the key to a positive outcome. Make the time for family. Let us stop replacing mom and dad with the cell phone. Be present, if at all possible. Instead of Facebook, You Tube, iPad, and television; let's try soccer games, little league, and ballet classes and family dinner for our entertainment. Execute better time management; you'll be amazed at how much you can get done in a day's time while getting to know your family better.

➤ Forgive.

If you don't forgive yourself, how can you

forgive others? It is a gift to you when you forgive. You are no longer held in a personal prison when you forgive. You should shield yourself from becoming damaged goods. To accomplish this, make sure to detach yourself from harmful persons and situations.

➢ Forget the past and enjoy your freedom.

I've found that the best way to get rid of the past is to:

- ❖ Have a conversation with yourself
- ❖ Write it down
- ❖ Read it
- ❖ Discard it

Do this every morning; it takes away the power of your past.

➢ Let it go!

It all begins with you, the man in the mirror. Remember, once and for all, get rid of the negative person, **you**!

Nutrition and Fitness

Chapter 19

Nutrition and Fitness

I notice every day, more and more people ask me if I am a trainer. I look that good? Thanks. On the other hand, the man in mirror; that's another story. That's the Virgo, again; perfectionist, another relationship killer.
I'm not on a diet; I just make better food choices. It is one of the greatest decisions I've made. It has been proven; good health brings less stress.

I've SEEN PEOPLE BIG and SEXY ORDER A LOT FOOD. Yes, a lot! They even know the song.

"May I have a Big Mac, Fillet-O-Fish, Quarter Pounder, French fries, icy Coke, milk shake, sundae, and apple pie."[9]

And, out of nowhere, with a DIET COKE? Please, this is when tension and weird looks begin. What's up with the diet coke? Yeah, yeah, I know you love the taste.

People, EATING A TOMATO ON A HAMBUGURGER IS NOT a salad.

Our food is poison.

FDA, WHAT ARE YOU FEEDING US?

Oh, I FORGOT, the FDA Doesn't WORK for the people.

Profit over human rights.

Think about it. How many people you know died last year from cancer?

It's the food, the water, and the toothpaste.

The number one culprit is how we process stress. It may seem that there's nothing you can do about stress. The bills won't stop coming. There will never be more hours in the day. Your career and family responsibilities will always be demanding. But, you have more control than you might think.

In fact, the simple realization that you're in control of your life is the foundation of stress management. Managing stress is all about taking charge of your thoughts, emotions, schedule, and the way you deal with problems.

How do we do this?

> Change your diet.
> Exercise daily.
> Learn the word, NO. (Let people deal with their own problems.)

- Laugh more. (Comedy Club)
- Work less. (Let people deal with their own problems.)

Wealth is based on the family. One of the craziest remarks I've heard is, "Fake it 'til you make it."

So, in other words, you shop to look rich, instead of saving to be rich.

I have seen women walk around carrying a $1,000 purse, with only $20 inside of it. I prefer it the other way around; having a $20 purse, with $1,000 cash inside of it. That's just me. I'm calling your name. I'm talking about you. Yes! Yes, you.

More Advice from J. Patrick, Esq.

Chapter 20

More Advice from J. Patrick, Esq.

Decision making is an art form. I think everyone has been faced with impulse buying. Instead of making an impulse decision to make a purchase, try this first. I got this idea from a comedian, a long time ago. Don't ask who because I don't remember.

One day I was impulse spending for a vehicle. As I was shopping, I began to sing this song by Kenny Rogers.

> "You've got to know
> when to hold 'em,
> know when to fold 'em,
> know when to walk away;
> and know when to run."

Come on, sing it. Yes, it is corny; but, it works. Sing it with me. Alright, I hear you. Now that's what I'm talking about. Taking the time to sing this chorus allows you the opportunity to delay your impulsiveness. On the other hand, the best thing to do in this particular situation is to take the time to write down the pros and cons. If the pros outweigh the cons, then it is a good decision. If the cons outweigh the pros, then it is a bad decision.

For instance, let's take a look at buying lottery tickets. What if $400 is spent per month on them. The harsh reality is, if you're not winning monthly; you're losing. I have a better idea. Wouldn't it be more feasible to take the $48,000.00 ($400/month X 10 years x 12 months) and put it in some type of savings account over time, be it long term or short term? The lottery is a game of chance. A savings account, Certificate of Deposit (CD), or some type of investment fund is more secure and promising than lottery winnings that are dependent upon selecting the right combination of numbers. You can think about it. You will thank me later. (You're welcome.)

As if impulse buying isn't enough, we have to deal with peer pressure to keep up with the Joneses. One of the craziest

remarks I've heard is, "Fake it 'til you make it."
So, in other words, you shop to look rich, instead of saving to be rich.

I have seen women walk around carrying a $1,000 purse, with only $20 inside of it. I prefer it the other way around; having a $20 purse, with $1,000 cash inside of it. That's just me. I'm calling your name. I'm talking about you. Yes! Yes, you.

Wealth is based on the family; not in the things that you possess. Build a stable and secure home with love, peace, joy, and a little common sense. Make a budget, stick to it and live within your means. You will see that you will have more money than you ever thought you could attain just by being practical and wise.

The Truth

Chapter 21

The Truth

The relief of the truth is like a bird departing from your soul. The loss will be great; but, your burden will be forgiven.

Society judges a man by the perception of the truth, rather than the actual character of the truth.

What is the truth?

The powers that be would rather promote a lie.

A little white lie satisfied the agenda, "the crime of all crimes", no crime.

Go to any courtroom in America. The

guilty could be found innocent; and, the innocent could be found guilty due to their representation in the weight of gold.

In some cases, you will see the light. That light will be control. We are plagued by profit over human rights. That's the bottom line of calculated exploitation. It's so hard being poor like me.

Walk with me and learn the Truth, He said.
Spirituality is something that is a journey deep within.
The journey to rightness is frightening to the enlightened.

The enlightened is one that accepts who they are.

Walk with me and learn the Truth, He said.

My struggles came with a lesson.

My lesson came with my teacher.

My teacher was life.

Walk with me and learn the Truth, He said.

Truth of the spirit or truth of the flesh is an everyday struggle.

Sight with no eyes is based on spiritual truth (faith).

Living with experience is based on physical truth (your understanding).

Perception is based on your understanding of the truth (pride).

Ha, ha, ha!!!

One-day tomorrow, it will be as clear to you as night and day (in death).

Walk with me and learn the Truth, He said.

Now I am confused as I walk with Him.

My understanding is based on the physical and perception of the truth.

That's the truth.

The truth is the truth of the truth; and, nothing but the truth.

Enlighten Me Not

Chapter 22

Enlighten Me Not

Enlighten me not with words of lies;

Amidst your inaccuracy of my history.

Is it true or not?

Teach me not.

What is your hidden agenda?

Is it true or not?

You wear the devil's tongue very well, I see.

Is it true or not?

Lie to me not.

Promise me not.

Should I have comfort?

Is it true or not?

Don't you understand the number one Golden Rule[10]?

Is it true or not?

Deliver me not.

Where are we going?

Is it on the map or not?

Is it true or not?

I know the road is hard, dusty and long; but, He made us strong.

That's the truth; but, you are not.

The devil always lies.

Understanding The Seven Deadly Sins

Chapter 23

Understanding The Seven Deadly Sins

I played with the devil in the journey of my life.

Understanding the seven deadly sins[11]; but, it came with a price.

Eating the forbidden fruit; it was a real challenge of life.

This mighty challenge is not for the light-hearted.

Born with free will; it came with the burden of the flesh.

Now, I understand why the devil envies us.

We are the only reason he has life.

He lives very deep within us.

If our relationship with God is strong, we will become the devil's master.

So, deny his whisper. Deny his cry. Deny him his glory.

He has no rights.

The true reason of life is the journey to the Light.

Everything is embedded within us. It's not in a picture; it's not in a place. It has nothing to do with tradition.

It has nothing to do with a symbol.

It has nothing to do with the Book. (The Basic Instructions Before Leaving Earth.)

Focus on your relationship with Him (within).

To be born a rock is just a rock that has no growth.

To transform into a rock, you will have to understand the process of becoming a rock.

The only friend of my enemy is me.

"Be careful of your decisions."

Lust shows you the weakness of your will. (Wanting something not of His will.)

Greed shows you your weakness of abundance. (My Unnecessary possessions are unnecessary burdens. Why should I worry about gold, when all I need is silver?) In other words, if you're stranded in the desert, what's more important: your weight in gold; or, a gallon of water? Think about it before you answer. Really, you're stranded in the desert. You can only live three days without water. Gold is a lifestyle; money is a tool. Don't be whores for it; take your power back.

Gluttony shows you your weakness of indulgence. (You should eat to live; not live to eat.)

Anger shows you your weakness in self-control. (Never release the beast that's deep down inside of you. Never give someone the ability to antagonize your power and take it away. Self-control is a precious gift.)

Envy shows you the weakness in your lack of focus. (When you focus on your own journey, you have no time to envy someone else's. It would be easy to take lessons from that person. Everyone needs a mentor.)

Sloth shows you your weakness in maturity. (Laziness; a person who doesn't work should not eat. John Crow[12], the scavenger of society. If you're an enabler, you sin as well. You're taking their ability to be free.) Fishing poles are great gifts.

Pride shows you the weakness in your lack of humility. (Entitlement; you will never see God's glory. The fallen angel was very prideful in his belief of being god.)

The seven deadly sins; don't embrace them. Don't give them any power. (They lurk inside our thoughts. "…Your thoughts… become your destiny."[3]) (Quote by Mahatma Gandhi)

Don't believe in God because the transition of death scares you.

Believe in Him because He's the Truth.

Journey well my brothers and sisters. He's waiting for you.

I Believe in You

Chapter 24

This chapter is dedicated to my grandmother, Elizabeth "Jane" Lewars.

I Believe in You

One of the greatest moments in my life is when I was able to change a negative situation into a positive one.

It started off with a simple whisper.

I believe in you, I'm not a liar.

I believe in you, I'm not a liar.

He spoke to me and said, I lived and I died for you.

Your burden is mine. Your worries are mine.

Never forget I'm always there from your first breath until your last.

I know your original name. I'm waiting for you to come home; but, there is work for you to do now.

CXVII

I believe in you, I'm not a liar.

I believe in you, I'm not a liar.

A warm sensational feeling came over me; and, the tears started falling.

I never felt peace like this before. "For God so loved the world, that he gave his only begotten Son, that whosoever believeth in him should not perish, but have everlasting life."[13]

Now, I understand what true love is.

I Win

Chapter 25

I Win

I don't win because of my ability.

I win because I don't give up.

I am a simple man with a purpose.

Life will place a monkey wrench in your path every time.

Use it to build your character.

Most of the time, envy lurks like a shadow, just like the wind.

Have you ever noticed?

The mountain stands strong. The wind must obey His strength.

Bobbing and weaving is a child's game. Be true to yourself.

That's when GOD smirks and says, "That's my people."

Walking and Content

Chapter 26

Walking and Content

Today, I really understand how to be happy and content with a simple life. I didn't have a ride to the gym today. So, I walked; and, then caught the bus.
I haven't caught the bus in a very long time.

Being one with nature and listening, you can hear the music from Mother Earth.
It is such a beautiful sound. While the other people rush about the day; I'm simply walking and content.

Saturday's Child

Chapter 27

Saturday's Child

Hello.

I am a tool.

I am Saturday's child.

Obstacle is my friend.

Nothing is easy for me; so, I adapt.

My headache is everyone's blessing.

Twenty-five Years and Still Crying

Chapter 28

Twenty-five Years and Still Crying

Twenty-five years and still crying.

I had a visitor in my dream today.

I never saw his or her face before.

I was young and not ready.

For thirty pieces of silver, I sold my soul, equaling ($ 350).

I aborted my child on the wish of the mother. After this, I hated her.

I hated myself because I was not able say, no.

Are you crazy? Twenty-five years and still crying.

One of the greatest gifts to be given is life.

Now, I am cursed and crying.

My seed has been destroyed.

Twenty-five years and still crying.

I will see you soon. Daddy is sorry, literally.

Home, Sweet Home!

Chapter 29

CXXVIII

Home, Sweet Home!

I was watching the news one evening.

There was a headliner on the beheading of a group of men who accepted death gracefully because they would not renounce their faith.

They died with a smile on their face knowing they had been true to themselves and to God. Most people saw the horrific act of it; but, I saw the beauty in it.

Now, I question myself. What would I do?

Would you choose life over your faith?

Most of us sell our souls for far less (99%).

This body is not mine. My hands are held by another.

I am a condemned man under the Guillotine; a simple

servant in the mix under the blue sky waiting patiently to go home.

Home, sweet home; a place where my flesh dares not to go. I am a spiritual man among the wicked. I am waiting to be completely free.

Freedom is the state of being at liberty rather than in confinement or under physical restraint. In this form, I'm in bondage.

As I am waiting under the blue sky, I faithfully accept my fate as a tortured soul.

Release me from this world and grant me a safe passage into my Father's bosom.

As I yearn to be free, the Guillotine drops.

Thank you, I am free now. The light is beautiful; I am home.

CXXX

So many wars are fought in the name of God. In actuality, they are fought over tradition and money. Tradition has nothing to do with the truth. One would say, "My father and his father went bowling; so, my son will bowl, too." I would rather know Him in my heart, than in a quoted scripture.

I AM NOT THE AUTHOR, JUST THE VESSEL.

My Famous Quotes

1. Power does not lie in a body of water. It lies (flows) with the river that has a purpose.

2. Remove the rock from Mother Earth. Tree must fall; the erosion of the family.

3. Don't give me a fish. Give me a fishing pole so that I can eat tomorrow.

4. Your lies and hidden agendas don't define who I am!

5. Did the sun rise or did the sun set? Neither, the world just turned.

6. Enemies are born by situation. Haters are born by lack of ability and envy.

7. Hate me! Makes you a better person. "You're welcome!"

8. Easy to sell your soul; hard to buy it back.

9. Someone asked me today, "What's the meaning behind the shirt?" I told them, "I'd rather fix the leak, instead of telling everyone it's raining cats and dogs."

10. Bi-polar Happy!

11. I Am Racist Against Racism.

12. The truth is the truth of the truth; and, nothing but the truth.

13. Happiness is when you don't need anyone's approval.

References

[1] Wikipedia contributors, "SMART criteria," *Wikipedia, The Free Encyclopedia,* https://en.wikipedia.org/w/index.php?title=SMART_criteria&oldid=671662248 (accessed July 23, 2015).

Doran, George T. "Management Review." What Is a SMART Goal? | Acronym Smart Goals. November 1, 1981. (accessed July 23, 2015.)

[2] Wikipedia contributors, "I Shot the Sheriff," *Wikipedia, The Free Encyclopedia,* https://en.wikipedia.org/w/index.php?title=I_Shot_the_Sheriff&oldid=671174991 (accessed July 23, 2015).

[3] Notable Quotes, "Mahatma Gandhi Quotes," *Notable Quotes.com,* http://www.notable-quotes.com/g/gandhi_mahatma.html (accessed July 23, 2015).

[4] Wikipedia contributors, "Bob Marley," *Wikipedia, The Free Encyclopedia,* https://en.wikipedia.org/w/index.php?title=Bob_Marley&oldid=670814573 (accessed July 23, 2015).

[5] Wikipedia contributors, "Black Lives Matter," *Wikipedia, The Free Encyclopedia,* https://en.wikipedia.org/w/index.php?title=Black_Lives_Matter&oldid=672560246 (accessed July 23, 2015).

[6] Wikipedia contributors, "Thin Line Between Love and Hate," *Wikipedia, The Free Encyclopedia,* https://en.wikipedia.org/w/index.php?title=Thin_Line_Between_Love_and_Hate&oldid=654201580 (accessed July 23, 2015).

[7] Wikipedia contributors, "E pluribus unum," *Wikipedia, The Free Encyclopedia,*

https://en.wikipedia.org/w/index.php?title=E_pluribus_un um&oldid=671583105 (accessed July 23, 2015).

[8] Wikipedia contributors, "Jerry Springer," *Wikipedia, The Free Encyclopedia,* https://en.wikipedia.org/w/index.php?title=Jerry_Springer&oldi d=670404464 (accessed July 23, 2015).

[9] Wikipedia contributors, "Big Mac," *Wikipedia, The Free Encyclopedia,* https://en.wikipedia.org/w/index.php?title=Big_Mac&oldid=661 091693 (accessed July 23, 2015).

"Big Mac." Wikipedia. 1974. (accessed July 23, 2015.)

[10] Wikipedia contributors, "Golden Rule," *Wikipedia, The Free Encyclopedia,*

CXXXVII

https://en.wikipedia.org/w/index.php?title=Golden_Rule&oldid =671110325 (accessed July 23, 2015).

"You Version Passage: Matthew 7:12 - King James Version." You Version. (accessed July 23, 2015.)

[11] Wikipedia contributors, "Seven deadly sins," *Wikipedia, The Free Encyclopedia*, https://en.wikipedia.org/w/index.php?title=Seven_deadly_sins &oldid=672087696 (accessed July 23, 2015).

[12] Pancocojams.Blogspot.com, "What 'John Crow' Means in Jamaica," *Pancocojams.Blogspot.com*, http://pancocojams.blogspot.com/2012/09/john-crow-part-i-what-john-crow-means.html (accessed July 24, 2015).

CXXXVIII

[13] "You Version Passage: John 3:16 - King James Version." You Version. (accessed July 23, 2015.)

[14] J. Patrick, Esq., "My Journey", *Real-life experience,* (The beginning through current, 2015).

Readers' Quotes

#1

"It keeps my interest...depicts a person trying to find them self.   Just wow...........five STAR."

#2

"The [passages] make you confront the reality of life today and make you remember the days of old when life was more simple and quiet. Makes you realize that love in life is very necessary. We can do a lot more than we think we can if we just keep moving and doing." ~ I.C. Hogan

#3

"I was expressing in conversation that I don't read poetry; but, much to my surprise I realized that the book was much more than poetry." ~Mr. Michael Phillips

#4

"You have very strong points of view. And the book makes the person reading it stop and go hmmm...interesting. You look at things in a whole different perspective which a lot of people are scared to do. Good job!"

#5

"I have had the pleasure of meeting the author. After reading his work, I have a formidable respect for his ability to go from abstract to deep thought throughout this book. The author's ability to draw me in to the material makes a huge impact. I definitely want to see and read more of his work.

This book would be a great self-help or inside thought process through self-absorption and healing."

~Sincerely, Professor L. Arno

#6

"An honest, thought provoking and emotion evoking work of written expression. Written from a man's perspective; but, can be enjoyed by audiences of both sexes." ~Sergio F. Figueroa

#7

"Jay, I enjoyed your book very much. In such a short read, I found laughter sadness, joy, self-esteem, empowerment; and, much, more. I had to read it twice because I can't believe how much of a POWER PUNCH you packed in your book... THANK YOU." ~Sofia